©2021 The Forecast Corporation

The Forecast Corporation
8 The Green
Dover, DE 19901
www.theforecastcorp.xyz

Like the world spins, so do the tables turn.

,
FS

CHAPTER 1

THE 17

The engineer asked jokingly, "You got any more?"
"I got sixteen left in the chamber." I answered.

"Can you hear yourself Anonymiss?" the engineer pressed a button from behind a window resembling the bulletproof, Chinese store glass and I could hear him in my head phones. "Yes," I said as I smiled in surprise to hear myself too. Singing the theme from the Smurf's, I sang in the mic giggling like I was at an amusement park. "Let's do a run through" he said. The Dragon Ball Z instrumental played and I began to rapidly sing. "I let y'all have y'all turn can I shine now somebody better let me in now y'all got money to burn can I get this couple dollars while that beat right there is breaking you in." Without stopping, I sang the song from beginning to end only catching my breath at the very end with a very loud exhale. The engineer was shocked that I had clearly sang this fast paced song with so many lyrics in one take. He asked, "You wanna hear that back?" What was meant to be a test run turned out to be the first recording of the first song that I ever wrote. I had written a rap when I was about five and a poem for a school assembly when I was sixteen. Now in college, I was intrigued into picking up the pen again by a local rapper who asked me to sing a hook on his song. It was the first time I heard a recording of my voice and on that day I was reborn. I don't know how I was existing before but I suddenly had vision, passion and freedom from an ordinary life of school, work, home, repeat.

The engineer asked jokingly, "You got any more?" "I got sixteen left in the chamber." I answered, knowing I only had fifty minutes left in the session before my sixty dollars ran out, I "tornadoed" through six more songs and time was up. I went into the control room behind the glass and swiveled like a child in the chair and watched the engineer "burn" my songs onto a CD. I asked, "Can I come back?" He said, "Yeah, you got something, I don't think I've ever had a session with an artist that recorded that many songs and they're all good, but what you're doing is like Karaoke. It's good for your first time but you need backgrounds and bells and whistles. Artists don't usually sing the songs straight through like that unless they're on stage." I was taken aback. I couldn't believe what he just said to me. He called me an artist! For the first time in anytime, someone acknowledged me as something I had no idea I was. I don't think I slept that night. I went to sleep with my new music playing on my iPod and woke up with my ears red and in excruciating pain from sleeping on the hard plastic headphones all night.

I found it super hard to focus at school or work now that I had a CD of my own music to listen to. I had dreams every night and day dreams every day about singing my songs on stage in elaborate "Cinderella-like" gowns. I remember going to a Thanksgiving dinner at my aunt's house and singing my new songs to my cousins. I was always the one who sang at the family events but after singing "Amazing Grace" or "Jesus Loves Me" at the main dining room table for my grandma, aunts and uncles, I was singing my songs for my cousins at the kitchen table, "I wish someone would please tell me what is going on, can't you see that things are crazy. Something must be wrong. I wish I had a dollar for every minute I wasted on you. I'm thanking God it's over and I am in a new place without you. You can't tell me that it don't hurt inside to see I'm not in love with you. You can't tell me that it don't hurt your pride." We would keep a look out because my family didn't allow "Rock and Roll" music. I was always a rebel though. I remember being in church at night service at about 4 years old. The deacons were singing and because my dad was a deacon he sat me in the front so he could watch me while he sang. My best friend at church and I started doing "New Edition" moves in the front of the church to a gospel song called "Whisper a little prayer". The church was trying not to laugh. My dad was making the referee gesture for "safe" to us while trying to stay in step with the male chorus and one of the missionaries came over trying to hide her smile and said, "Cut it y'all". When we got in the car my dad said, "Don't you EVER do that in church again. You are something else!" Night services were always more fun than morning service.

I stayed a block away from campus and always had friends over. It was a never ending party. With school and my new passion as an artist, while everybody was dancing, drinking and smoking, I was in another world studying C++, Lao Tzu and Sigmund Freud while humming melodies, after which I'd be dancing, drinking and smoking. Now we were dancing to my music. I had written about all my friends and our crazy weekends in one of the songs called "Friday". One line sang, "I gotta get to Toppers first, so stressed I'm boutta burst my stupid day at work had me so mad I cursed". Toppers is an exclusive spa in Philly. I've never been but I hear it's nice. The hook said,"Get your gear together call all the girls around cuz tonight's the party let's tear the city down. Call your man and tell him that you'll be back by three if you wanna party come on and roll with me".

My sister, Kesha who owned a chain of salons came over one day and heard my CD playing. She said, "Who's that!" I answered, "Me." She didn't even ask, she ejected the CD, took it and left. Next thing I knew I had a new manager or executive from a label every three weeks promising to "blow me up" but after a certain point, I was left to figure it out on my own. There was a guy who worked for the promotions department at Sony who came to Philly and took me to meet with KayGee of Naughty By Nature and I left the meeting excited to hear back but nothing came of it. I decided to try to do things on my own so I would just go to different studios and wait around until I could get in on a session. Doing this, I started picking up steam around Philly so I dropped my classes and started using a childhood name I got in a bussing battle in elementary school, Frankie, and a friend of my sisters who I briefly worked with said my lyrics were Stormy, so I chose the name Frankie Storm. Everyone seemed to be wowed by me, but things never worked out and I felt like time was running out as doors would close whenever I wouldn't sign my life away in the bad deals that were offered.

Almost two months went by and I was planning to pick my courses back up when I got a call from the top producers in Philly at the time, Dre and Vidal, a production team that had produced for the likes of Michael Jackson and Kanye West. I might've been at the studio before we got off the phone. It was like Grand Central Station in there. I was a guppy in an ocean. Dre and Vidal were rarely ever even at the studio, but the little time they did have to devote to me was needed and appreciated. They taught me about the business side of music and introduced me to Wardell Malloy, my point person at the performing rights organization, Broadcast Music Inc., better known as BMI. These are the people who collect royalties for musicians. I signed my contract with BMI and I hadn't even written any songs with them yet. I would go there every day and watch the greatest artists and songwriters in the world come through. PoohBear, Ryan Toby, Floetry and Boyz2Men would all just be writing and hanging out all the time. Who knew that all of this greatness was right up the street from me. I never forced my way into a session. I spent a lot of the time in the TV room playing PlayStation. Nobody was hurting for lyrics or anything. Everything changed when I met a songwriter named Balewa Muhummad who was also a giant in music. He had credits with Mariah and Whitney just to name of few. He asked me "You got something on this?" When I got the chance to write with him he said to me, "You're dope, you need to get a deal." I asked what a deal was. He went on to explain what publishing was and how I could get an advance from a label for it. With that information I made music a new course of study. At the next session, Balewa invited me to a session in New York to write for an artist signed to Atlantic Records. It was my first time in Manhattan. I used to spend summers at Saratoga projects in White Plains, New York with my aunts and uncles so I'm sure we passed it but never stopped. I was still pinching myself from months back because of my first times in the studio but now I was sure I was dreaming. I drove a Ford Contour. It was a blue car with a red door. I parked it in Newark, New Jersey to avoid the pricey parking in Manhattan and took the train one stop to New York. Balewa had me in a nice hotel, all expenses paid and when we went to the studio we had "runners" kind of like assistants who would go get us whatever we wanted. We had a food budget and we ordered the best food in New York and while I saw everybody throwing their food out, I took a doggie bag to the hotel every night. On my down time, I called every label in New York with my only pitch being. "I wouldn't be wasting your time if I didn't know I was hot." I spoke to assistants, interns and security praying I would get a meeting. The last day of the NY sessions was underway when in walks a short, thin, white man that everybody seemed to know and be fond of. He said hi to everyone and then asked the runners to order him some oxtails and plantains. When the other writers and producers asked "what you know about oxtails?" His reply was,"I'm probably blacker than you." Everybody laughed including me. An hour or so passed and I was in the main room by myself when the oxtail eater came in and said,"I'm hearing you from the other room, sounds pretty good. I'm an entertainment attorney. What are your goals?" My reply was that I wanted to be the next version of another writer. His counter was,"Call me when you want more." After blowing my mind with his response, he handed me his card.

The sessions in NY were over and so was the hotel stay but I wasn't stopping until I at least got a meeting. A few labels said they would call me back. Before we parted, Balewa passed me the phone and said, "Somebody wants to speak to you." It was KayGee. He said, "Hey Frankie, I got a few projects I'm finishing up. Come through and vibe out with us and we can work on your stuff too." I hugged Balewa so hard. I didn't even know he knew KayGee, but why wouldn't he. They were both top tier in the music industry and I found out fast that there were only few at that level. I went back to Philly to check on my house and drove to Orange, NJ almost everyday for the sessions with KayGee. I met Treach and Vinny, both amazing guys. Another one of my favorite people at Divine Mill (That was the name of KayGee's studio) was Freeze. Freeze didn't produce or write or anything that had to do with music, but he believed in me like an older brother. I remember after taking a meeting with Virgin records to become an artist I was paired with another artist to write for her. I brought the project to KayGee's spot and because I had gone so hard up to that point, I got sick. So sick that when the artist's A&R came to get the single, I couldn't write and my voice was completely gone. Well, Freeze looked at me and said, "No, you are gonna get this done." I've seen you write too many big records for you to fumble on this one. He left and came back with a bottle of Hennessy and heated it up and put a shot in a mug for me. He said drink this. This is a Hot Totty. With no voice or strength, I drank it. In the next 10 minutes, I wrote and sang what would become the artist's first single. "I'm Not Missing You" by Stacie Orrico. In the original recording, you can hear the raspiness and nasal tone in my hoarse voice.

Rob Herrera was KayGee's engineer and my absolute best friend at the time. He was the one I had all the inside jokes with. He taught me what a good recording should sound like and what a true friend is. Rob started engineering really young under the great, Bruce Swedien, who we recently lost. Rob has worked with all the greats. You can't get him to say it but you name them, he's got credits with them. KayGee's studio was so star-studded. I couldn't begin to remember everybody who came in there. I remember Red Rat the reggae artist came in the main room and said, "Ay you girl inna di tight up skirt" and I said, "Ya make mi head swell til mi blood vessel burst." I was like, "Oh shit!! That's Red Rat!!. It was nonstop laughter and hits. Kay didn't like everything but when he did, you knew it was a go. One day Kay brought in a track and said, "See what you can do on this for Jaheim." Rob loaded it up and the lyrics came straight away. "I'm not wilding out like I used to. I don't do the things I used to no more. I've changed for you." Kay said, " That's it!" That song went on to become a single, co-written by Balewa, with Jaheim featuring Keyshia Cole and they left my voice on the hook. Kay asked me if I wanted to put my name on the song as a feature too but since I hadn't started on my album yet, I said no.

I finally got a call from two labels but they were days apart. I believe one was on a Tuesday and the other a Thursday. I drove my blue car with the red door to New

York for the Tuesday meeting and to avoid the pricey parking and hotel costs, I slept in the car until the Thursday meeting. I was so close to having everything I ever prayed for so having to start the car a few times throughout the night to get the rats away didn't deter me in the slightest. Besides I kept a pet mouse in a peanut butter jar when I was small until my dad found out and threw it in the sewer. I looked out one night and saw one by itself and wondered if it was trainable but then the rest of its family came and I quickly deleted that thought, started the car and turned up the radio. Because of what I was there for, sleeping in my car was no different from sleeping in the hotel. I was sleeping under the New York sky, minutes away from the best food and shopping in the world and hours away from meetings with the greatest music corporations in existence. I had God, my music and a few believers. I had beaten the odds.

CHAPTER 2

THE PURSUIT

"You don't need to worry about people not working with you. When you're hot they'll find you under a rock."

I arrived in New York. First things first. Where will I park this car and not get towed? These signs are so confusing. Do I follow the red ones or the green ones? Or the green ones unless the red ones say something different? I couldn't ask anybody cuz they would ignore me or they didn't speak English. I finally found a park and now I was so far away from the label that I need to get a taxi. And I'm feeling like Dorothy from "The Wiz" because every driver is passing me by. I knew from the Atlantic sessions to start out an hour early because of the non cooperative Taxi service and I wasn't confident enough in the subway routes to take that. I finally made it to my Tuesday meeting with Jake Ottman at EMI.

Jake Ottman had signed a group called The Fray who were good friends with Stacie Orrico, so he knew all about the work I had done with Stacie and that I was in talks of doing a deal at Virgin Records where Stacie was already signed. EMI was somehow the publishing company attached to Virgin Records.

Jake walked in minutes after I was escorted to his office by his assistant and if music was a person, it would be Jake Ottman. Good music was the only thing that moved him. Everyone else I had run into wasn't quick to show emotion when they heard a good song but he was unafraid to show that he loved something when it was really good. He played me some of the new music that The Fray was working on and it was phenomenal. He cared nothing about the politics of it at all. He thought my songs and my music-ability was great and he made me feel like I had made his day when I came to see him. Some of my music had arrived before I did, so when I started to play a few songs, he would comment at the start. I was so taken by his care and attention. In the middle of about the fifth song, Jody walked in and she got right to business. She asked me where I was from. I said, "Philadelphia" She told me how she liked Philly and said, "I'm hearing great things about you, Frankie." She looked at Jake and said, "Lets take her to Marty." I went to Marty Bandier's office and ransacked the candy jar. Everyone smiled and after speaking with Marty about what I had done so far and what I wanted to do from there, Marty asked, "Who's your attorney?" I said I don't have one. He said, "Well, you better get one." I said, "I will right away!" The meeting was over and I skipped twenty-five long blocks all the way back to my car. I had a few bucks so I found the nearest steak spot to celebrate. I went to a Starbucks to freshen up and charge my phone and went back to my car when I got a call from KayGee that Stacie was coming in to record "I'm not missing you," so I headed back to New Jersey to meet Stacie there for what would become my first vocal coaching session. She was a pro so it didn't take long to get it done. The only part we really had to coach her on were the ad libs. Rob and I said, "Do some ad libs." I did a little ad lib run and Stacie said, "Oh you mean like Justin Timberlake?" We thought that was adorable and she nailed it. If you've heard it, let me know how I did. Yea, you!

I gassed up and headed back to New York, repeating the parking process on Wednesday morning around two AM which was much easier because everyone had gone home I guess. I parked, got in the back seat under my comforter and went to sleep. The next morning, I did my Starbucks bird bath and wandered around Manhattan the whole day with nothing to do but wait for Thursday. Balled up in the back seat of my Contour, I slept the day and night away. Thursday was here! I had a meeting at Universal Music Group with Ethiopia Habtemarium, Andrew Gold and Ross Donadio. Andrew and Ross absolutely loved the diversity of my music and Ethiopia was all in. Once she knew that my goals were to be an artist and do publishing in the same company, her very firm response was, "I get it, let's do it!" EMI was so interested in me they sent me on my first trip to the west-coast! I was going to meet Jon Platt better known as Big Jon. The meeting was scheduled on a Saturday. This was a first. No one was in the office so he had to send a runner around back to get me. I came in to his massive office and sitting in a giant art deco chair was one of the tallest men I've ever seen but in all his tallness, he was such a gentle spirit. He didn't have an industry vibe at all. He was ready to hear what everybody had told him about me. He is now the Chairman and CEO of guess where?? Sony Music Publishing formerly known as Sony/ATV!!! He recently told me that I was the only writer he ever took a meeting with on a Saturday. Yay me!!!

Back to the story, I played him the few songs I had on my phone and he liked them. I knew the EMI meetings had gone well because they offered me a deal. Once I got the first offer, every label and publishing company wanted to sign me. In my mind at the time I didn't want to offend anyone in hopes of working with everyone. It was the best problem I ever had. One label rep, Tanya Brown invited me to the studio on the epic night that Jay-Z and Rodney Jerkins were there. It was the night Jay-Z was recording his verse on "Déjà vu". What she told me quickly dissolved my indecisiveness. She said, "You don't need to worry about people not working with you. When you're hot they'll find you under a rock." After the first two meetings I got calls from four more labels and every time I would go and play my music, I had another offer. Wanting me to stay close, the label executives would ask where I was staying and I would say the cross streets where my car was parked. When they would ask what hotel was there, I would say, "My car." Needless to say the car and I soon had other options. Every label rep I met offered me a place to sleep. I stayed everywhere from penthouses to The Plaza hotel and I was introduced to just about every A-list celebrity on the east-coast at the time. Everyday became a celebration; good food, expensive atmospheres and new opportunities. I was next to the most powerful people in the music industry at their requests. I got black cars from one corner to the next to make it to meetings and sessions. The meetings made me feel like royalty. I was offered black cards, shopping sprees, a son's hand in marriage and loads of cash. I had started a bidding war over a ninety-three pound girl from North Philadelphia, literally fresh off the streets and green as neon.

My point person at BMI, Wardell Malloy got wind of everything that was going on and he invited me to a listening event where I could play my music and get feedback from the audience. I went there and I felt like I was back in college except everybody there did what I did. Meaning they were all musicians in some form. Some were writers like me, others produced, some played instruments. There was also a conductor there, he conducted an actual orchestra. When I got up to play my music and said I was from Philly, there were two girls in the front row from Philly too. I never did get their names. Once I took a mental survey of who was in the room, I said in my head, "Fame!!! I'm gonna live forever. I'm gonna learn how to fly, ahhh!!!" Once again, on the top floor of some billion-dollar building, eating the best food and rubbing shoulders with the most creative people on the east-coast. I felt extra special when Wardell had me and just one other producer hanging with him the whole time and taking us into the exclusive off-limit areas of the building. There was champagne and talks of bright futures. I left the event swirling in amazement. I attended my next few meetings with the extra charged battery that Wardell had ever so fabulously placed in my back. He told me that I was genre-less, that I was one-of-a-kind and I acted accordingly.

After all the meetings were done I went back to KayGee because even though I was on the brink of a deal he was allowing me to get sharper. I always had the main room when I came and I was knocking songs out the park and I loved it there. KayGee came in the main room before he was leaving one night and told me he signed a group in Miami and he wanted me to come to Miami and write with them. I really fell on the floor and was like "I'm going to Miami!" He said, "So I guess that's a yes? Give Dede (His sister) your info and we out Friday." I picked myself up and ran down the hall and gave Dede my info for the plane ticket and hotel.

Off to Miami we went. When I landed and left the airport, the warm air felt like oil on my skin! I said in my head, "I belong here!" Once again I'm in an amazing hotel on South Beach. Tramp, another producer at

Divine Mill took me to get sushi for the first time!! And not just regular sushi, It was a "take your shoes off and sit Indian style at the short table" sushi place. I overdid it on the wasabi for the first time and Tramp thought it was hilarious. After he was done laughing at me, he gave me a thorough run down of everything on the menu and we tried just about everything. I was hooked on sushi after that. The Japanese ladies saw me everyday after that for almost the whole trip. It was time to do the ceremonial Miami walk down South Beach and I was ready. I had on a half shirt some tight jeans and strappy sandals just purchased from a boutique on the beach. I ran into some people I went to church with growing up. When they saw me, the only girl walking with a bunch of heavy hitters on South Beach, they were proud of me. We hugged, said see you back home and parted ways. We stopped at a restaurant and I ate seafood. The seafood on South Beach was like triple what it costs in Philly but it was an experience and so worth it.

We had a session in a studio on Collins but it was more so for Kay and Tramp to make beats for the other sessions coming up. The next day, KayGee introduced me to film producer, Shakim Compere who just so happened to have a spare penthouse in Coconut Grove that he let me stay in for a night because Hurricane Katrina had rolled through Miami and driving back to South Beach wasn't safe. Riding on the way to Shakim's house was super rough. There were light poles and trees falling right in front of us. I forget who was driving, but looking back he probably saved all of our lives. His maneuvering game was sturdy. I just remember covering my head and every time I looked up something else was falling around the truck. KayGee and the rest of the guys had suites at the Grand Hyatt in Coconut Grove. So I guess they left and went there after I fell asleep.

After surviving the storm, I woke up the next morning and wrapped myself in a sheet, rolled up some paper like I had a long cigarette and went over to the window and role played like I was a debutante and I was talking to my chef. "Yes, I'll have the Crepes Suzette and poached eggs for breakfast, merci." Kay called, it was studio time. We drove back to South Beach, I got dressed and we went to the studio. Not just any studio but the most exclusive spot in all of Florida, the legendary Hit Factory. The halls were filled with platinum and gold plaques from everybody who's anybody and the rooms were filled with state-of-the-art everything as far as equipment. We rocked out for a week on the second floor in the room all the way down the hall . I did all my writing on the balcony. The weather was always beautiful and my level of creativity heightened while I was there. It was total paradise. The engineers and runners were the best in the business. I would go back in the studio when I was ready to record with the group and they would change things around to fit what they were feeling and they would take turns going into the booth to record their parts. I had never worked with a group before so it was dope to see how four guys could have four different personalities, four different vocal ranges, be totally interested in four different life styles and make one song that sounded like one voice. They were hilarious too. I think one of them liked me too. He gave me his jacket when it got a little chilly and when it was time for me to leave he said he would come get his jacket later but I gave it to him right then and went back to my hotel. I never saw them again after that but we had a great rapport. When I got out of the car Kay said we're leaving tomorrow, be ready at eleven. I said, "No!!!!!" and ran in the hotel. KayGee had to nearly pry me off the hotel pillar the next morning because I didn't want to leave but back up top we went.

I went back to Philly to regroup and I had various sessions that the labels I took the meetings with had set up for me in New York. Even though I hadn't signed with anyone, they started showing interest right away. I was packing to head back and out of nowhere I got a call from a production team that I worked with months prior called "The Matrax". I had done some songs as an artist there. They were calling to tell me that they played my songs for a label A&R at Sony Canada and the label wanted to release them on one of the biggest artists in Canada. I couldn't believe that another situation that I thought nothing would come of turned out to work in my favor. It was not just one, but three of my songs with none other than Canadian artist, Keshia Chanté. We won a Juno award (Canadian Grammy) for "Been gone" and I got invited to do red carpet with wardrobe and diamond fittings in Canada, but I couldn't go because it was last minute and I still had other obligations at hand. Three of the songs were with The Matrax but the final song I got on Keshia's album was written with none other than Balewa Muhammad in the first New York sessions he invited me to weeks before. It wasn't originally written for Keshia but amazing that it made her album.

Off to NY I went with more great news but I was still torn between what company to go with. They were all so perfect. Not knowing where to start when choosing the label that would become my musical home brought me back to the conversation I had with the attorney where he told me to call him when I wanted more. I gave him a call and my first words were,"Hi Todd, this is Frankie Storm, I want more." He laughed and asked what was going on. I let him know the companies I had meetings with and the people who were there and he knew all of them. He began reaching out and the offers started to climb over each other. Almost passing out as the agreements leaned in my favor and the numbers grew, I kept my mouth shut and let my attorney do his magic. Yes, I made him my attorney post haste. I had every major label and publishing company ready to take me on in whatever capacity I wished, all I had to do was say yes. After receiving six contracts and going back and forth in negotiations for 3 months, I was down to two choices. Sony/ATV and EMI. Sony was a boutique company with way less writers than EMI which had a humongous roster with countless writers and producers. Being new to the music industry, I felt that individualized attention at Sony would be needed. Another perk was that I would be signing with the company that Michael Jackson was half owner of. The only catch with Sony was the president at the time didn't want me to pursue an artist career. He said it would distract me from writing, while at EMI they wanted me to be an artist because they felt it would maximize the publishing. What should I do?

CHAPTER 3

THE DEAL

"I'm trading my book bag for a suitcase, I'mma hustle my way up outta this place."

I signed a 6 figure, 4 song publishing deal with Sony/ATV music publishing. This meant that I had to place 400% worth of material. Let me explain. A song writer usually contributes 50% of a song and the producer the other 50%, so I would have to place 8 songs at 50% each, adding up to 400%. That would be affected by the amount of writers and producers contributing to a song or if there was a sample in the song. The shares would change according to the percentage the other participants and/or the owner of the sample wants.

The meeting for the contract signing was just like I had imagined. A long conference table in a plush office on the 5th floor of the Sony building on 55th and Madison Ave. At the table was my attorney, Todd Rubenstein, the person who brought me to the label, Rich Christina, the president of the label, Danny Strick and little, tiny me. I had no placements at the time, meaning I had no songs on the radio. The deal was based on my potential alone. We went page by page and Todd explained everything to me line by line. I signed, scratched and sniffed where needed and it was a done deal.

The night I signed I was taken to dinner at one of the most exclusive restaurants in NewYork, Nobu, by Rich and Todd. They were good friends who went to college together. We walked up a wide staircase onto a level which looked like a VIP section. There were chandeliers everywhere and all I could hear was the sound of expensive dishes and low chatter. When I turned to admire the layout of the restaurant, Sean "Puffy" Combs was sitting at the table next to us!!! I immediately got nervous because he was outside of the TV, an arm reach away. I said in my head, "Don't fan out Frankie!" Everything became a blur. Everything started moving in slow motion. My napkin fell off my lap, I reached down to pick it up and when I sat up, a waitress came to ask me whether I wanted still or sparkling water. Thinking this exquisite place would only have sparkling water coming from its faucets and Still was the brand name. My response was,"Still sparkling's fine." Rich leaned over and whispered," Still OR sparkling Frankie." I laughed and said,"Sparkling's fine". Todd, my attorney did the ordering. We ate the thinnest slices of sashimi I had ever seen but man they were "get take-out everyday for the next two weeks" good. My sushi addiction continued. Just then, Puffy and his guests got up to leave. My anxious angel was screaming, "Tell him you got that work!!" While my fall back angel was saying, "Nah fall back." I let that one get away but I said in my head, "Never again!" The night ended, but not before I was gifted a 20 year old bottle of Dom Perignon. With my contract in my book bag and my bottle of Dom in its elaborate gift bag, I headed off to my hotel stopping to enjoy the New York lights on that warm summer day in July. I returned to my room to stay awake all night calling everyone who I thought would be happy for me.

After those two calls, I wrote a song called "Dreamer Ways". The song starts off "I'm trading my book bag for a suitcase, I'mma hustle my way up outta this place. To a new city, I'll be a new face, where everything's for the taking yo I can't wait." I had just signed with one of the largest corporations in the world, I had more money than I ever had before and I was staying in one of the most historic and exquisite hotels in the world. I thought to myself, I gotta get a nice pair of shades for this blindingly bright future of mine.

The first session I was assigned to, after signing with Sony was with the Norwegian production duo, Stargate in which I wrote the song that would change the sound of music at the time.

CHAPTER 4

DON'T STOP THE MUSIC

"I wanna take you away. Let's escape into the music. DJ let it play."

The location was Battery Studios, 2007 and I was officially a writer on the roster of Sony/ATV music publishing. I walked into the main room and even though I had been in a good amount of sessions, none of that prepared me for this one. I had heard so many great things about Stargate's music but nothing about them as personalities. One of them was signed with Sony/ATV and the other with EMI, so getting to work with both of them was a fulfillment of what Tanya Brown had spoken into existence weeks before. In walks two super tall men from Norway. One named Tor and the other Mikkel. There wasn't much small talk at all. They began playing tracks. I chose the very first two they played. I started with the first one. It was an interpolation of "Personal Jesus" by Depeche Mode. The name of the song I wrote to that track was "Rock and a Hard Place" It said,"I'm stuck between a rock and a hard place. Can't move, can't stay. I know I gotta go but I don't know which way. Don't wanna leave me don't wanna hurt you. Stuck in the middle goin in circles." Stargate approved! They changed it around some, I recorded it and we were on to the next track. The second track I wrote to was a Stargate-style track. If you know anything about their music, you'll understand exactly what I mean. It was a mid tempo with their signature snare pattern. "Cry" was the title I selected for this one. The hook lyrics were, "This time was different. Felt like I was just a victim and it cut me like a knife when you walked out of my life now I'm in this condition and I got all the symptoms of a girl with a broken heart but no matter what you'll never see me cry." They were pretty reserved guys so I really couldn't tell if they were excited about anything. The fact that we kept cutting songs was my indication that I was doing a good job. We recorded "Cry" and we were about to take a break to eat. They said someone wants to speak to you on the phone. I thought it was Rich. I came to the phone and said, "Hello." The guy on the phone said,"This is Jay Brown, I hear you in there doin ya thing" I said, "Thank you!" With the biggest smile on my face. Still so new to the industry, I had no idea who Jay Brown was, but I would soon find out because he wanted to meet with me. I ecstatically agreed to the meeting, ended the call and we ate lunch. I'm sure I had sushi.

It was time to get back to work. This next track came like it was hidden in The Arc of the Covenant. There was no briefing beforehand. The only preface was that the idea for it came from the president of Roc Nation, Jay Brown, and it would be for Rihanna. They pressed play and it sounded like disco. I hadn't heard disco since my mother played Donna Summer when I was small. Then, an all too familiar voice sang,"Heehee! Woooohoo!" This track seeped into my soul like no other track ever. It was so perfectly crafted that I felt like a 5D chess player came into the room and challenged me to a match. I said, "That's Michael Jackson! Can we do this? Is that legal?" They said, "We will have to get it cleared but, yeah." They left me alone with the track and after about three more plays, I felt like the room wasn't big enough for me and this track to have a proper bout, so I went out into the streets of New York, with the instrumental recorded on my little dictaphone. I took the track to a bar where we danced and drank shots and then we went on a tour of Time Square. It was time to go back to my hotel and while staring out the window at the view I just left, lightning struck. I would end up writing a recap of my night to the track. The first verse started, "It's getting late. I'm making my way over to my favorite place. I gotta get my body movin' shake the stress away." The track being so big and having Michael's voice on it had me stressed out. I was signed with his company and I was not about to let him down, knowing he was gonna hear this. "I wasn't lookin' for nobody when you looked my way, possible candidate, yea." I was speaking reminiscently about how everybody wanted to sign me and that Sony/ATV was one of the possible choices. "Who knew that you'd be up in here lookin' like you do. You're makin' stayin' over here impossible." I couldn't stay in the studio with a track so massive, I had to get out. "Baby I must say your aura is incredible." Speaking about the spirit of the track and how it brought me back to when mom would play Donna Summer. "If you don't have to go, don't. Do you know what you started? " Tributing to the "Wanna Be Starting Something" sample in it. For the rest of the first verse, I felt like every good dance song needed instructions and the rest of the verse lyrics would be prophetic of the impact the song had on clubs around the world. "I just came her to party and now we're rockin' on the dance floor acting naughty. You're hands around my waist. Just let the music play. We're hand in hand, chest to chest and now were face to face." The hook was a recap of me taking the track out into the world first stopping at a club to get inspiration. The hook sings,"I wanna take you away. Let's escape into the music, DJ let it play. I just can't refuse it. Like the way you move it. Keep on rockin' to it. Please don't stop the - Please don't stop the music.

The sun was coming up and I didn't realize so many hours had passed. Studio was at 1pm and I didn't wanna go to sleep in fear that I would oversleep. So I went to get breakfast and wrote the second verse at the restaurant. "Baby are you ready cuz it's getting close? Don't you feel the passion ready to explode?" I was feeling the pressure of the session approaching not knowing what they would think of the song. "What goes on between us no-one has to know this is a private show, oh." All the while I was disguising my experience under what would sound like a meeting on the dance floor to the listeners. It was 1:15pm. Time to go.

When I arrived to the session, TyTy, an executive from Roc Nation was there. He came to the studio to hear the song I had written. I had always heard his name in Jay-Z's songs but never knew what he looked like. He was a beautiful guy, inside and out. With big brown eyes and a smile that let you see clear through to his heart. He said, "Let's hear it." I wasn't even nervous singing in front of him because I felt like I knew him because in my head Jay-Z and I were related somehow. After I sang it, TyTy said, "That's it. Record it. Just like that. Don't change nothin." I smiled and said, "Thank you." Stargate said, "Let's do it." I made some tea, killing the honey bear, and went in the booth. Getting through the song was fairly easy. I had learned what they expected in the vocal from the first two songs I recorded with them. We started with the hook and then recorded the verses and pre-hook. The most complicated part to recording that song was re-singing "mamase mamasa mamacosa" over and over again. My lips were numb AF, but it was a smash! What a great first session!!! I knew without a shadow of a doubt in my mind that song was a hit.

I had many great sessions with Tor and Mikkel after that. The one that would stay with me the most was the session where I met Rihanna. Rich called and said, "Rihanna is recording the songs you wrote and they want you to come and write some more." I was like "The songs, like plural?" He told me they were keeping two of them. I'm like "Sheesh! This just keeps getting better." Sony made the arrangements and I would be leaving the following week. I was home packing, but this time I was packing for LA, so I had to do it with a different approach. I got every half shirt, bralette and booty short I had in my repertoire. I went to the mall and got 2 pair of shades: One Dior and one Gucci. I had a fresh Louis duffel, a Tiffany necklace and bracelet set and my diamond stud earrings that I only wore twice before. For the feet, I got two fresh pair of Giuseppe heels and some pink Givenchy gummies to lounge in. I got a mani-pedi and some fresh bundles installed and I was on my way to LA.

With time to spare, I stopped at a restaurant in the airport to get, of course, sushi!! I was getting a lot of tracks from producers all over the world as word about my writing got out. As I ate, I listened to the tracks and came up with melodies and concepts for them. Writing the rest of the song was always easy for me. I got a to-go box and went to my gate to board the plane. I remember I had a window seat. The reason I remember was because after I realized everything that happened over the past couple months and where and what I came from, I began to cry like a newborn, with my head against the window. The lady in the aisle seat asked me what was wrong and I said,"I'm just happy". She said, "Well you just keep on crying." I'm about to cry again right now. Hold on…

The flight attendant came by and asked me if I was ok and the lady in the aisle seat answered her and said, "Oh she's just happy that's all." The attendant said,"That's great! Awe, you're gonna make me cry." The aisle lady said ,"I know, me too!" The attendant came back with tissue for me, the aisle lady and one for herself. It was awesome. I landed in sunny LA with an extra dose of power from the skies. I felt unstoppable. The first session was that day so I went to drop my bags at the hotel and off to the studio I went. I was greeted by the staff at West Lake studio and they took me back to where Stargate was. They had two studios running and they situated me in one down the hall to the left. I had on a green sweatsuit and I was sitting at the control board writing a song. In walks TyTy and announces

Rihanna's coming in. I want you to meet her. I'm like she's coming in here or you want me to go out there? He said, "She's coming in now."

In walks Robyn Rihanna Fenty, and I was ready to be taken aback by this diva like specimen so I braced myself but to my surprise she was like, "What's up girl! You nice with the pen I hear!" I sank in to my chair and laughed like I was being tickled. She asked, "How long are you staying?" I answered, "As long as I can! " I told her I was writing another one for her right then but when I was about to sing it for her, TyTy came in and said Tor and Mikkel were waiting for her to go record in the other room. So she said, "Be back" and the next time I would see her would be a few hours later across the hall. Mikkel pressed play and out of the speakers came Rihanna's recording of "Don't Stop the Music". As TyTy danced around the studio, you couldn't tell me I wasn't on a cloud. My mind was racing a million miles a minute and all I could say to her was,"Thank you" and I told her how amazing her voice sounded. Then they pressed play again and "Cry" played in her voice and I did my Tyra Banks sniff up to stop the tears. Everybody said, "Congratulations" to everybody and I left the room and went back across the hall.

After everything settled, Stargate and TyTy wanted to hear the new song I had written. "Colours" was the name of it. Listening back now, it captures the mood of that day so well. It went,"The sky was perfect blue, me and you with a new beginning. One and one made two all we knew is that we had each other. Like gentle lavender on my face what a gorgeous feeling you took me up so high felt so free with no walls or ceilings. For every way my emotions have gone there's a shade that goes along. Your painting of me like the canvases your portrait my song. Went through so many changes, don't know how I became this. There's a different shade for all that we've been through. These are my colors for you. I'm tryna think back to what I was before you. But for every turn, a different hue. These are my colors for you. " If you see my pattern of inspiration, you know exactly what I drew from when I wrote those lyrics. After I finished singing the song, TyTy pointed at me and said, "You got something special." I had then left the cloud I was on for outer space.

The next day I came in, I was walking down the hall to get to the lounge because it was past both studios. Jay Brown and Rihanna were standing in front of the first studio that I was writing in. Rihanna said, "Hey hotty!" Trying not to geek out, I went to touch her hand as if to gesture, "Girl you are about to make me blush." I missed her hand and touched her leg and oh my stars!!! It felt like the softest satin, hand-crafted by deities. I kept walking but I had to look back to make sure that was skin I touched. She had on a green, mini dress that stopped just below the belt, and yes, it was all skin. I wonder if Fenty Skin has that formula in it.

Stargate called me into the room where I had heard the new recordings the day before. I recorded "Colours" and the LA sessions with Stargate were done. I did a few other sessions with other producers and flew back on the redeye that night.

CHAPTER 5

THE TOUR

I said, "What is this I'm stepping on?" He had the nerve to say, "That's Chinchilla."

After that session, I went on a national songwriting tour. With an unwavering determination to succeed, the first year in my publishing deal I only took 5 days off. The only downside was every time I went to a session I would get asked why I wasn't an artist. Two new labels offered to sign me as an artist after I signed my publishing deal with Sony, Virgin Records and Disney(Hollywood Records). Lawyers were involved both times to seal the deal but it seemed that every time my label got wind of it, the offers would go away.
I went everywhere from Washington State to Florida and every musical place in between. My music traveled further than I did. I had songs playing all over the world getting synch requests almost every week. I was not in

or around the music industry before, so while others had knowledge of key players and possessed a certain etiquette, I knew nothing of the lingo or how to hide my passion.

The next producer Rich sent me to work with was Steve Morales. The way Rich described him was no match for what I encountered when I arrived. He came to pick me up from the airport in a white Bentley Flying Spur and as if that wasn't dope enough, when I got in and put my feet on the floor it felt like the floor melted. I said, "What is this I'm stepping on?" He had the nerve to say, "That's Chinchilla." I was like, "Stop this car, I will walk from here." He smiled. I took my shoes off. As we pulled up to his, what I thought was a house, and the gates of his Coral Gables mansion opened, I froze. "Are we on the set of a new movie?" That's what I said in my head. Everything was marble and glass. The whole house was controlled by one huge remote. He had the nicest studio I had ever been in with a white SSL board. In all my five months of writing, I had never seen a white SSL board and it had a Vegas function that made it light up with all the rainbow colors. He had a full production team there working and it was all kept in order by the lady of the house Danielle. She is all the makings of a queen. With a house full of Latinos, she kept everybody orderly and made sure all the guest were comfortable. With all the luxurious things Steve had, none of it matched the magnitude of his catalogue or the diversity of his newly created music. I could see why Rich sent me there. Steve was genre-less like me. He could produce for any artist, new or vintage.

After the tour and Danielle showing me to my quarters, we got straight to it. He played seven tracks, all dopeness. Because his personality and the atmosphere inspired me so much, I said, "I'll write them all." He loaded them up. I sat inside the booth on the floor with the headphones on and started on track one. When I was done I found him in the house, wherever he was, and he came to listen. He was like, "That's fire! You ready to record?" I wanted to write them all and then record the next day. He was blown away. He was like, "Ight!" and that's what I did. He couldn't believe that I could write so many songs in one session and they were all great. I know that's how he felt because he was on the phone telling somebody that. That somebody was his good friend, Enrique Iglesias who Steve and I worked with shortly after. We all wrote the Euro Cup song "Can You Hear Me" for Enrique after that.

Enrique was so fond of my writing he called me back when he was working with another producer, Red One, which led to me writing two more songs for Enrique, one with Akon, "One Day At a Time" and the other has the greatest story. Enrique, Red One and I were in Jim Henson studios in LA. We were writing a song for Enrique's album. He said I think this one needs a feature. He asked, "You know anybody hot that can feature on this?"

Mark Pitts was an A&R at Jive Records. He has just been promoted to President of RCA Records. Congratulations Mark!!! He had just called me to do a session a few weeks back with Ciara. I wrote a song with a dope producer named Syience called "Fit of Love" for her. I was like "Ciara would kill this." Enrique said, "Call her up." So I did and she brought her sweet self to the studio and nailed the recording and the video of "Taking Back My Love". Enrique performed both songs at the Euro Cup. Ciara joined him for the second song. I was at Record Plant studio and I had just been introduced to Kanye West thirty minutes prior. He was in the back eating nachos and when I walked back toward him, he gave me a once over and said, "You wrote Don't Stop the Music? That's the shit! We should get in." I thanked him and told him I loved his music and I would love to work with him. Then I quickly turned and walked away because inside I was losing my lunch and I didn't want to start sweating in his nachos.

In between the Enrique and Ciara sessions, Juan Madrid, another executive at Sony set me up on a session with Disney(Hollywood Records). The A&R I worked with was Allison Hamamura. Now that I had seen many projects being put together, I was in awe that every project I worked on with Allison had a clear direction and if the record was going to have twelve songs on it, we were cutting fifteen at the most. She wasn't a budget pillager and she took care of me as a writer. She would call me in, brief me and let me go to work. I worked on several projects there but the most dear to my heart was Raven Symone. Being one of the most outstanding figures of this lifetime, I couldn't believe how human she was. Every time she would record, her warm up song was "She Will Be Loved" by Maroon 5. She was so easy to coach and took direction so well, I kept forgetting she was her! We spent about two weeks at Glenwood Place studio putting her album together and it was part of a soundtrack for "College Road Trip," the movie with her and Martin Lawrence. We had conversations about and outside of music and when she wasn't making me darn near pea my pants laughing she was just being a genuine, sensitive female. Another iconic person Allison introduced me to was one of my favorite artists growing up, his name is Kwame. I had no idea that he was a producer. When I walked in, I expected him to at least look a little older than I remember. But nope, he hadn't aged at all and he was sharp as needles. We worked on other Disney projects and landed a song on a double platinum album with Australian artist, Jessica Mauboy titled "Up Down".

I was back home because I was planning to take a vacation in Miami for my birthday when I received two separate emails from Sony. The first one was for splits. Splits are the breakdown of the percentages for the contributors to a song. This split request was for a song that I co-wrote, "Hold It Don't Drop It" that would soon be placed on Jennifer Lopez. It was a single on her "Brave" album. She would later say in an interview that it was her favorite song to perform. The second email was Sony confirming the percentage that I had on another song "The Cure" which I wrote for a reggae artist named Jah Cure.

Changing my number once a month made it difficult to get a hold of me if you weren't Rich. In a session at Electracraft with one of my favorite engineers, Will Garrett, I got a visitor. It was Jeff Fenster, who I'd met a few weeks back at a session with Pop Wansel and Oak Felder at Harvey Mason's studio. Speaking of Pop and Oak, we wrote, "Only Wanna Give It To You" by Elle Varner featuring J. Cole, "Never Always" by Charice, an

Oprah protege signed to Warner and we also penned "After Party" and "Tears" for, Letoya Luckett.

Back to Jeff. He said, "Frankie, I've been trying to get a hold of you, who is your manager?" I said, "I don't have one." He paused, looked at me and said, "I'm going to be your manager, come to my office in the morning and we'll discuss it." I was so happy. Jeff was the "King of A&R" and he earned that title. This book would go on forever if I named all of his accomplishments in music. I went to his office the next day and the meeting went so well we hugged to seal the deal. Before Jeff and I had our conversation, there was someone who I met at a Sony writing camp. He would call me and ask what I was doing for the day. It was always a session so he would show up and take care of anything I needed. This went on for weeks. I was at a session with The Orange Factory when Jeremy, the founder of the company asked what's up with this guy. He seems to be hanging around a lot. I didn't have an answer. So I took the guy in the hall and asked him what was going on. He said, "I'm just here to help you out. I see you running around by yourself and I wanted to make sure you was good. That man's name is Ryan Press and I ended up choosing him as my day to day manager and introducing him to Jeff because Jeff was at Warner and wouldn't be able to move around with me like Ryan could. The tour continued, Sony would set 'em up and I'd knock em down. Ryan was the one who introduced me to Kanye West and set me up on the impromptu sessions with Oak and Letoya Luckett.

We were in LA, I forget what we were working on but I know Brandy was there in another session. Yup! The woman with the most distinguishably gorgeous voice you've ever heard. She saw me and knew who I was too! She said, "Hey Frankie! We need to get in." I'm in my head like, WTF! Sony's word of mouth promotion strategy is second-to-none. Later that day I got a call from Brandon Creed, who was Brandy's A&R at the time. He was calling to give me Brandy's number. I gave it to Ryan to set up the session. Next thing I know they're engaged! I saw them at a Jill Scott concert a few months later and they looked so in love. Ryan ended up taking a job with Warner Publishing and managing me would be a conflict of interest so we had to part ways. I was already used to running things on my own so it wasn't too bad but not having someone so on top of my schedule reminded me that it was ok to take a break. I flew to Miami just to take a little down time and see what it was like without an entourage and appointments. I stayed at the Biltmore in Coral Gables and what a get away it was. I finally got to go on the beach and enjoy the Miami night life. "Don't Stop the Music" was playing everywhere!!! I was driving on the highway in Miami and it was on in the car next to me and they were going off! I never said anything to anyone but just watching people's reaction to it was such a gift. I was thanking God every time I heard it somewhere. I had already fallen in love with Miami but to know that I was a little part of creating the atmosphere made me love it even more.

I flew from Miami back to LA because I was scheduled by Theresa LaBarbera Whites to do sessions with Dr. Luke and Benny Blanco for Britney Spears. These sessions were what I had always imagined the rock star life was like. They were at Conway Studios. The place was so big, and I've never rode on one, but I heard they provided scooters to ride around on. I do know first hand though that there were free flowing margaritas and fresh baked cookies nonstop. Whatever your pleasure, it was there. Dr. Luke was a speeding bullet of energy and Benny Blanco was just the opposite and it made for a great team. I was in Britney's room before she arrived and my phone rang. It was Eve. Yes, Eve from The Ruff Ryders. The "Brick-house Stallion" from Philly. She was doing a song for the "Transporter 3" soundtrack and she wanted me to "spark it off". I wrote a hook and bridge to a song I called "Set It On Fire" and sent it to her in minutes. Oh! I almost forgot, as I was writing the soundtrack song for Eve, in walks, none other than, Chris Brown. He said, "Hi, I'm Chris!" I was like "I know! Hi! I'm Frankie!" He said,"I know! You in here writing that fire?" I was like,"You know it!" He said,"I'm in the other studio if you need any help" I was like "Bet!" He left as quickly as he came in. I went looking for him as soon as I came to my senses but he was gone. Damn!

Eve recorded the song within the next few days and we got the slot on the soundtrack. All this while waiting for Britney to grace us with her presence. I went across the way to see if Luke and Benny had any tracks for me to start on, and they did. We began writing to a Prince-like vibe. "French fingertips, red lips, bitch is dangerous. Cotton candy kiss can't wait for my sugar rush. Can't take it no more. I got to have more tonight. The feeling's so strong I'm putting you on tonight. All right, let's go". Working with those two was a totally different vibe than any other session I'd been in, but I think that was the idea. I was being groomed to work in various vibes. Britney came into the room where we were. This was at the time when the media said she was spiraling downward. I didn't see that at all. She appeared to be a humble, hardworking girl who loved music. She was so meek that when she came in, she was the only one in the room standing and with tall heels on, I'm sure she wanted to sit down. I said,"Britney, you wanna sit down?" She said, "Yes," like she was about to fall down and as she took my seat, I left the room because I was overwhelmed by her demeanor. I learned quickly that a lot in the music industry is not what it was made to seem like. We named that song for Britney "Lace and Leather" and that would become the song that Britney did her strip teases to on stage for the tour. Those sessions went so well that Luke called me back to work with him at his house.

Being in LA and having my car slide backward down a hill, already being afraid of heights, is the most "unfun" part of being in California. I could not go to Luke's house alone. Jeff had to drive me up those hills damn near blindfolded. Where he lives, there are not only rollercoaster, steep hills but there are narrow roads where a slight miscalculation to the left or right will have you falling thousands of feet down to "roadkillville". I couldn't understand why people would want to live in houses that were supported by stilts.

Ok, back to Dr. Luke's house. It was a massive, multi-level mansion with a view of the entire LA. It was fit for a diamond selling hit-maker and that's what he is. He had a studio that if you asked me how to get to it I probably couldn't remember and it was in the same house. He was obviously fond of my writing but I think he was more impressed by my heart. He would ask me often,"How are you such a good person?" The only way I could respond was,"I'm just being me." We didn't always agree on everything like who would be elected president or if the world was more good than bad, but he treated me like a little sister and he wanted to see me win.

Rob Herrera, KayGee's engineer decided to move to Miami and he was quickly chosen by the Hit Factory as one of their main engineers. He previously worked at the Hit Factory in New York as a teenager and I believe the same people also owned the location in Miami. While I was there, I stopped in to see Rob and he introduced me to Slim from Cash Money Records. Not hearing much about Slim, I had no idea that he was the one behind the inner workings of the label. I played him some songs and he liked them. He would later call me in to do writing for the artists on the label. I would then find out at a session, to my surprise, that Tyga had used a hook I wrote named "Where Am I?" on his "The

Potential" mix tape. "I traveled the world, city to city don't know where I'mma stop and I wake up every morning like, where am I?" and he left my voice on the hook.

Slim encouraged me to grow my brand. He asked if I had any producers because I would run through tracks like water and be in the studio waiting for the producers to make more. I decided to sign the Matrax, Scott Carter and Dame Hayes. Grammy nominated producer and engineer Scott, who I named "Robot" because he's like a computer. My slogan for him was "Input data, output song." Damon Hayes is the drums of the pair. He has produced for just about every known rap artist there is, most recently producing "Green Gucci Suit" for Rick Ross featuring Future. We ran all over Miami and Slim gave us the green light to go all the way in on the projects. We had so much fun and got so much work done.

Slim came in on a rare occasion to hear the songs. He usually just had the engineer send them to him. After he listened, he told me which artist each song would be good for. He then asked if there was anything else I was working on. I had been writing with another production team called The Orange Factory in New York and they had an amazing artist named Jay Sean. He had a lot of overseas success but they were looking to launch him in the United States. I told Slim about him and that I thought Cash Money would be great to help The Orange Factory cross him over. Well, he said,"Set it up."and I did. Jay Sean went on to get his first number one on the US billboard charts and peak in the top five all over the world. It was also Cash Money's first number one on the Billboard Hot 100. And it was the opening song in the Karate Kid movie starring Jaden Smith. Not only was I invited to the Cash Money Grammy party that year but I had my own list. The producers I signed, The Matrax, were there and I think I even invited a princess of a foreign country. I made sure everybody on my list made it and then I came after. When I got there, the guards at the gate were like, "There you are!" We were escorted in on golf carts and we had our own section in VIP. It was an amazing night.

I had management before, but for the first time in my career, I met someone who wanted to manage me both as an artist and a songwriter. This force to be reckoned with is named, Aja Patterson. I had done a few sessions for the artists she worked with at Warner Music and after so many times of her saying, you should keep that one for you, because no-one could deliver them quite like I did, she started asking about me as an artist. She was the right hand to one of the most powerful men in music, Lyor Cohen. She was fabulous, draped in Chanel and diamonds and had access to all the artists and executives everywhere. She genuinely wanted to work with me because I was different and as she would say, "You are the undeniable Frankie Mutha-fuckin' Storm." "Frankie Pants" for short. When she began to handle my career, things went awesomely. She set up photoshoots, shows and had me dressed by the best stylists in the game. We sat with every big boss in the biz, including, LA Reid, who was the president of Epic Records and Rob Stevenson, the executive vice president at Universal Republic. Aja connecting Rob and I got me a massive placement. It was a mid-tempo called "Sorry to

Interrupt". It was recorded by the multi-talented, Jessie J, the adorable R&B songstress Jhene Aiko and Rixton, Scooter Braun's group from the UK. It was written over an interpolation of the 90's classic "Return of the Mack" and the song had its own tour and guess what the tour was for? None other than everybody's favorite grab and go breakfast, Pop Tarts!!! Cross marketing at its finest. Aja is now the right hand of the multi-faceted mogul, Nick Cannon, whom she also introduced me to. She invited me to a writing camp he was having in Atlanta. I rode down with, Shawn Burgendy, award-winning cinematographer and director of photography and editor of the hit, Lions Gate series Money and Violence.

I went straight to work when I got there. Everybody was apprehensive about what I could do, but once I start cranking out the Storm, they quickly understood why Aja brought me in. We left the studio and went to a strip club because you can't go to Atlanta without that experience and the food was phenomenal. I got back to the house and fell right to sleep. The next day we were back at the studio. After writing about five songs, Nick came in. He was walking past the studio I was in and then he doubled back and extended his hand. He said, "Hi, I'm Nick". I said, "Hey Nick, I'm Frankie" He said, "Thanks for coming." I said, "Thanks for having me." He said, "I got the songs, you are really dope!" with a super serious look on his face. I went into my tickle laugh and said, "Thank you, you're dope too!" He said, "Thank you, keep it up," and he went in the booth to record. When he shook my hand, I just knew this man had never touched a rough thing in his life. He might need to launch a skincare line too.

I spent a week working with his label, "NCredible". He had all the writers in a huge, fabulous house. The room I had was beautiful. It had a glass door entrance so I could see the sky at night. I was in Atlanta with Aja, Nick, his artists and his team. We recorded at Patchwerk studio, with Pink and Vern, two of the dopest engineers to touch a console, and we got it in! With Tre Boogie on the tracks and Bobo, the A&R making the play to the fullest, I filled up a full, yellow tablet with songs that week. When I wasn't working, I got to hang out on the set with Aja. I went backstage with the whole "Wild 'N Out" crew. It was a whole party back there; music, convo, food and drinks, the healthy kind.

There was an album release celebration for one of the Ncredible artists. We were like twenty cars deep and when we arrived in the club with Nick, the club announced that Nick was in the building and over came the sparkling bottle girls. They played the artist's music and we danced. After a few dances and a couple drinks, it was time to go. We left out the same way we came in, star-like. I returned home with another colossal notch under my songwriter belt.

With everything I've included in this chapter there is still more so I've included my discography at the end.

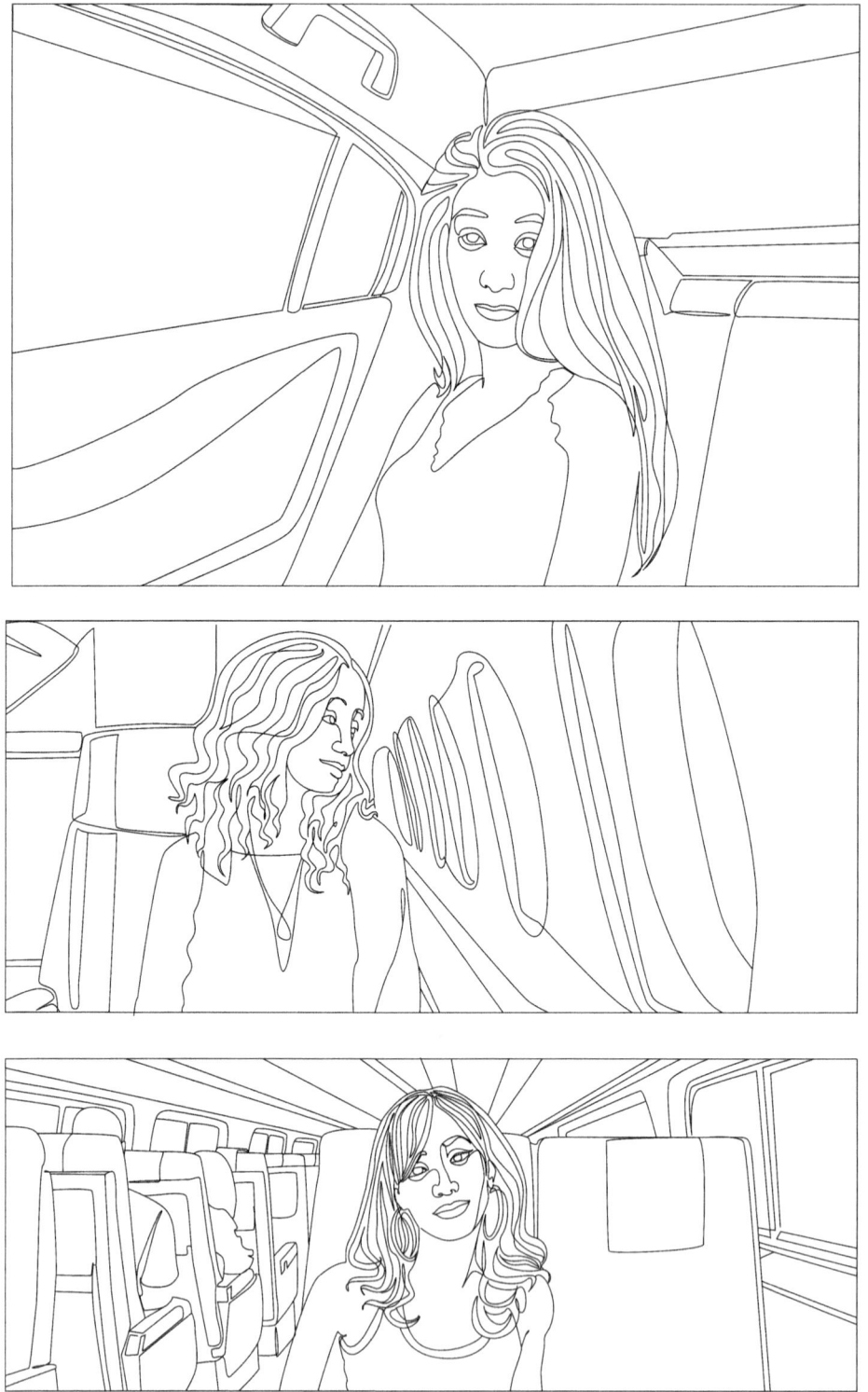

CHAPTER 6

THE NOD

"I was at home watching my favorite movie, Gattaca, when I got a call from Rich and Todd."

Let's rewind to around seven months into my first year writing, when I worked 360 out of 365 days. I was finally going to meet Jay Brown, RocNation president, at the Def Jam building. I was taken to the meeting by my manager at the time. He was the liaison between me and Sony for scheduling my trips and sessions. He told me before I went into the meeting that they were going to ask to manage me. He said he wouldn't mind doing joint management with them. I agreed and went into the building. In a massive office sat Jay Brown. He shook my hand and said, "I'm Jay Brown, nice to meet you Frankie. Whacha been up to?" My response was, " I signed with Sony/ATV and it's been nonstop ever since." He let me know that he was hearing great things about me and that Jay-Z was coming in to meet me. He ordered some food and got me a sandwich. I was eating, trying not to look as hungry as I was. He said, "That's why you so skinny, you don't eat nothin". TyTy came in and took me into his office where LA Reid came in and introduced himself. LA told me my musical reputation had preceded me and everybody in the building was excited about the songs that I had written for Rihanna. TyTy told me when Jay-Z heard "Don't Stop the Music" he said, "That's money!" Michael Jackson cleared the sample of his voice and I was told he loved the record also.

After about four hours in the building meeting just about everyone, and falling asleep on TyTy's office couch, I was taken back into Jay Brown's office. He said, "You know why you're here right?" I said, "Because of the songs?" He said, "Yes and we want to manage you". I told him that was awesome and my current manager was willing to do joint management. He didn't seem to happy about that. I don't remember how he expressed his opposition but I knew that was a no go. After waiting four more hours for Jay-Z to arrive. TyTy said he wouldn't be in until the morning, so I left. I called my manager and he came to get me. I told him what happened and he said, "That's what happens when you're the hottest song writer on the planet." My sadness went away and we went to a session where I wrote a song called "The Show Must Go On". The lyrics were, "The world is waiting. They're here to see me, can't do them wrong. The show must go on and when I hear the crowd scream cuz they're playing my song they can't wait long, the show must go on".

The following Sunday, I got a short notice session for Monday morning and Sony was closed and didn't book day of tickets, so I got my manager to book me a ticket to New York. I got on the train as usual, writing on the way. This train ride was strange. For the first time they came through the train checking ID's. I gave them my ID and when they returned it, I continued writing. My stop at Penn Station was approaching and I collected my things and got ready to exit the train. When I got off, two officers asked me to come with them. I said, "OK" not knowing why. They took me to a police station in Penn Station and asked me how I got my ticket. I told them that my manager had gotten it for me. They asked me who it was and I told them. They said they were investigating a credit card fraud ring and my ticket was brought by a stolen credit card. I asked them if I was being "punked" but they assured me they were serious. They asked me about various people in the industry and still being so new, I didn't know anyone outside of the Sony system. They quickly realized I was innocent and asked who usually booked my tickets. When I told them my point person at Sony/ATV. They asked me to call Rich. I called Rich and he assured them that I had just signed with Sony and had no reason to steal a $50 ticket. He asked them to tell me to come to Sony after they were done talking to me. I called my manager and told him I hope he rots in hell.

I came in the building shaken up and Rich walked toward me down the hall smiling and said, "Frankie just got out of train jail!" I smiled, changed my number, gave it to Rich and headed to my session.

A few months later, I was called back to work with Stargate. I was thinking it would be a normal, hit-making, Stargate session but not this time. I was in the main room and in walked King Bey, one of the most amazing performers to grace the stage since Michael and Janet!!! She was so cute and little. The spotlight makes her look ten feet tall but to my surprise she was so petite. I shook her tiny, little hand and she said, "Hi, I'm Beyonce". I did a low scream because I didn't want to scare her and I practically ran outta there into the booth to write. I was just about finished writing the song when Tor and Mikkel came in the booth and said, "We want you to meet somebody." I walked into the main room thinking I was going to be introduced to an artist or executive and there on the couch sitting next to Tim Blacksmith, Stargate's manager, was the greatest lyricist and business mogul of this lifetime, Jay-Z. I don't know how fast I walked over to shake his hand but it felt like I was moving in slow motion again. He said, "Congratulations," speaking of the success of "Don't Stop the Music" and he told me about how he met and signed Stargate to RocNation, which they had newly launched.

I couldn't speak at all because I was in a daze. Every word he said had an echo and I nodded and agreed accordingly. After about seven minutes, I did manage to say that it was nice meeting him and I went back to work shivering.

I thought to myself not only do I have the hottest song on the radio right now but in the credits, my name was next to the greatest entertainer of now and forever, Michael Jackson, half owner of Sony/ATV, where I was signed. I had just met two of the world most recognizable household names, Beyonce and Jay-Z and I got to watch a rising superstar, Rihanna, sing the lyrics that came from my pen and the biggest producers in the world, Stargate. What more could I ask for? I'd soon find out.

Fast forward a few months later. I was home watching my favorite movie, Gattaca, when I got a call from Rich and Todd. When I picked up, Todd said,"Oh, You're just gonna do this right out the gate?" I had no idea what they were talking about. Rich said, "You got a Grammy nod!" I dropped my phone, screamed to the top of my

lungs and fell to my knees thanking God. I was satisfied at every level of success I had reached. Recording my first songs, placing my first song, hearing the songs I wrote play on the radio for the first time, meeting my first big artist, getting on a movie soundtrack, but to get nominated for a Grammy was something that wasn't even on my radar. I hadn't even started thinking about that yet, but there it was. I made the list.
"Don't Stop the Music" was slated to be an album cut. It became a single because it was chosen by the people and had grown so massively that the label decided to package it as a single.

After a super successful year and clearing the board of all of my musical goals, requested and unexpected, Rich came to a later Stargate session to tell me he was leaving Sony/ATV for a new position at EMI, go figure. After crying in his arms for the remainder of my session, I gathered myself and asked him who I would be speaking to since he'd be gone. He transferred me to the president of the company, Danny Strick. Things were awesome with Danny. The best part of it was his assistant, Regina "Reggie" Bosso. It was like I got promoted. Danny and Reggie made it so I had the resources to really start my own label. The only difference was they didn't warn me about the motives of people like Rich did. I ended up spending $128,000 on a project that I never saw any return on. I quickly recouped the loss from my own catalogue but I never looked at the music industry the same again.

I decided to take the revenue I generated from music and start investing. I turned to the family business, real estate. I bought several properties in Philadelphia. I loved going to survey and rehab properties and go to closings. Things were lucrative for the first year until the partner I had to manage the properties turned to drugs and we parted ways. Realizing how hard it was to manage the properties on my own and not finding reliable property management to keep the properties maintained, I ended up giving my properties away to family.

I then found a new passion as a teacher, using songs to quickly teach children all subjects. I would go to various neighborhoods and teach the kids that were around faster than their teachers. Some would end up teaching their siblings and friends. This became a new passion so I started The S.T.O.R.M. School, an acronym for The Science and Technology Outreach Music/Media School. Since then, I've created several inventions in the fields of communications, technology, clothing, and toys, holding several patents and trademarks.

You can succeed in entertainment or any other industry without doing anything strange. You just have to be extremely hard working and talented and not do anything strange. Being stealthy also helped me. I let my goals announce themselves and my accomplishments speak for me. I also turned down a lot of invitations that weren't in line with my spirit. See! I was able to do all of this without even sticking around for the pictures. 🤫

Discography (Random Order)

Rihanna - Good Girl Gone Bad
  Don't Stop the Music
  Cry

Michael Jackson - I Love MJ Forever
  Don't Stop the Music

Jessie J ft. Jhené Aiko and Rixton
  Sorry To Interrupt - PopTarts Commercial and Tour

Elle Varner ft. J. Cole - Perfectly Imperfect
  Only Wanna Give It To You

Demi Lovato - Unbroken
  Light Weight

Angel Haze - Dirty Gold
  Sing About Me

Kat Dahlia - My Garden
  Saturday/Sunday
  Mirror
  Walk On Water

Double (Japan)
  Lips

Chelley (Ultra Records)
  Love Sick

Tyga - The Potential
  Where Am I

Jah Cure - The Universal Cure
  The Universal Cure

Parade (UK) - Louder
   Light It Up

Enrique Iglesias - Insomniac
   Taking Back My Love

Britney Spears - Circus
   Lace and Leather

Jay Sean - All or Nothing
   Do You Remember

Jaheim ft. Keyshia Cole - The Makings of a Man
   I've Changed

Elliot Yamin - Fight for Love
   Always

Natasha - Sidekick
   Sidekick

Enrique Iglesias-Greatest Hits
   Can You Hear Me (Euro Cup)
   Takin Back My Love ft. Ciara

Enrique Iglesias-Euphoria
   One Day At a Time ft. Akon

School Gyrls - School Gyrls Soundtrack
   I'm Not Just a Girl

Jamie Cullum-The Pursuit
   Don't Stop the Music

Stacie Orrico - Beautiful Awakening
   I'm Not Missing You
   Take Me Away
   Don't Ask Me To Stay

Ciara - Fantasy Ride
   Fit Of Love

Anastacia - Heavy Rotation
   Heavy Rotation

Raven Symone - Raven Symone
   In the Pictures
   In Your Skin
   Anti-Love Song

Letoya Luckett - Lady Love
   Tears
   After Party

Jordin Sparks - Jordin Sparks
   Now You Tell Me

Jordin Sparks - Battlefield -
   Walking On Snow

Marié Digby - Breathing Underwater
   Avalanche
   Come To Life
   Know You By Heart
   Crazier Things Have Happened

Jessica Mauboy (Australia)
   Up/Down

Jennifer Lopez-Brave
   Hold It Don't Drop It

Miss Elva (Japan) - Miss Elva
   I'm Not Afraid

Rainie Yang (Taiwan) -
   It's Our World

Charice - Infinity
   Never Always

Eva Avila - (Canada) Just Gimme the Music
   Just Gimme the Music

Keshia Chante (Canada) - 2U
   2U
   Been Gone
   Sorry

Natalia (UK) - Perfect Day
   Perfect Day

Compilations

Kidz Bop Non Stop Pop

Lullaby Renditions of Rihanna

Stand Up and Cheer

Weekend Anthems

Verve Digital Free

Ultimate Pop Jr.

Sexy R&B: 40 Massive R&B Anthems

Reggae 2010

RMF FM Najlepsza Muzyka:

Now That's What I Call Music! 75

Now That's What I Call Music! 33

Kidz Bop Dance Party!

Kidz Bop 18

Barbie: Let's All Dance

Absolute Dance

YTV Big Fun Party Mix, Vol 10

Ultimate Pop Party

Just Dance: The Biggest Club Remixes

Club Land Classix, Vol. 2

Nick: Kids Choice Award Compilation

Movies and TV Shows

Britain's Got Talent

American Idol

Idol Gives Back

So You Think You Can Dance

Jennifer Lopez: Dance Again

The X Factor

Here Comes the Boom

Pitch Perfect

Demi Lovato: Stay Strong

The Karate Kid

Brothers & Sisters

America's Best Dance Crew

Confessions of a Shopaholic

Transporter 3

College Road Trip

Germany's Next Top Model

Brands

Sony

MTV

Universal Music Group

Disney

Warner Music Group

Nickelodeon

McDonald's (Toy iPod)

Pop Tarts

Cirque Du Soleil

Frankie Storm

As a Philly born, New York bred singer, songwriter, instrumentalist, inventor and teacher, Frankie has decided to add author to her repertoire.

www.ingramcontent.com/pod-product-compliance
Lightning Source LLC
Chambersburg PA
CBHW062144100526
44589CB00014B/1684